One thing I've learned over years happen. We have to be intentional in and intentional during our time in the word. This *Reflective Bible Journal* will help you daily lay your emotions and concerns before God to listen well and to let God shape your heart and mind through scripture.

— LISA APPELO, author and speaker

Many of us read the Bible because we think we're supposed to, but we stop short of connecting with God and his Word at a heart-level. The *Reflective Bible Journal* is a holistic approach to reading God's Word. Taryn provides an intentional guide that will not only lead you deeper into Scripture, but will also encourage you to bring your whole self, emotions included, into your Bible reading.

— JAZMIN N. FRANK, author of *Name Above All Names*, *In the Waiting*, and the *Devoted Scripture Journal*

I have a dozen journals on my shelf right now. But I will replace every one with the gift that Taryn Nergaard has created in her *Reflective Bible Journal*. This journal is more than just a place to write down your thoughts or record your day. Taryn has constructed a journal with thoughtful steps to strengthen your relationship with God, build your Bible knowledge, integrate God's Word into each day, and improve the relationships in your life. Its design encourages you to evaluate your current mindset, look for the places in your life where you may need to forgive or repent, and record the transformation as you go deeper in your relationship with God. This beautiful journal is perfect both for a new believer who seeks spiritual direction as well as for a long time believer who wants to be more intentional in their walk with Jesus. I will be giving several as gifts! Thank you Taryn, for this contribution to Christian growth and spiritual formation.

— BRIANE KEARNS, Bible study author, writer and speaker

Showing up before God as our true and honest self can be intimidating, especially if you have never done it before! Through the *Reflective Bible Journal*, Taryn teaches that we not only can approach God with all of our mess, but we can allow him to come in and change us through immersing ourselves in his Word. This journal is a lovely way to learn how to approach God through our time with him, and grow closer to him through his Word.

— EVA KUBASIAK, author of the *Deep Dive Journal*

Taryn Nergaard invites us to step into a wholehearted and intimate relationship with God through his Word. Designed for honest evaluation and reflection, this journal elevates time with God by encouraging the reader to reflect on all aspects of daily life and how it relates to our obedience to and abundance in Jesus. If you are looking for a thoughtful, honest approach to your quiet time, let this journal lead you there.

— THELMA NIENHUIS, author of *Quiet Assurance: Meditations on Peace for the Grieving Heart*

Taryn Nergaard's *Reflective Bible Journal* is a simple but profound invitation to intentionally and authentically dig into God's word and apply it to your life. This masterfully-crafted journal provides opportunities to read, receive, reflect, respond, and remember God's word and note all the ways he's working in your life daily, weekly, and seasonally. Taryn offers practical instruction on how to make the most of each part of the journal, so if you forget the point or purpose of any given section, just return to *Using the Journal*, and it's all laid out for you in an easy-to-read format. I find the *Emotions* section of *Resources* to be particularly helpful for pinpointing my emotions, which in turn brings greater self-awareness and closeness with the Lord as I surrender my life to him. May this journal be a blessing to all who use it.

— AMY BETH PEDERSON, author of *The Apple of My Eye: Trusting God's Guidance When We Can't See*

Does God ever seem distant to you? Does reading the Bible ever feel like trying to eat a stale cracker? Taryn Nergaard's *Reflective Bible Journal* will bring your time in God's Word alive and help you find new ways to connect with the Lord. I am confident that using this journal will usher in transformation and growth through the opportunities it gives you to receive, reflect, and respond. I've never seen a Bible journal like this! You're going to want a copy for yourself and all your Bible reading friends.

— KRISTIN VANDERLIP, author of *Life Worth Living: A Daily Growth Journal*

In a world battling for our attention, the *Reflective Bible Journal* invites us into a slower, more soulful time abiding in his presence. Taryn Nergaard provides a thoughtful process of Bible reflection, encouraging weary hearts to soak up the life-changing truths of Scripture. If you long to shift your gaze to the One who is worthy of your worship, the *Reflective Bible Journal* is an invitation into a deeper, more meaningful practice of spending time in God's Word.

— SARA WARD, author of *Made for Hope: Discovering Unexpected Gifts in Brokenness* and the *Made for Hope Bible Study*

typewriter
creative co.

www.tarynnergaard.com

Scripture quotations have been taken from the Christian Standard Bible®, Copyright © 2017 by Holman Bible Publishers. Used by permission. Christian Standard Bible® and CSB® are federally registered trademarks of Holman Bible Publishers.

Edited by Jennie G. Scott.

Cover & interior design by Typewriter Creative Co. Cover graphics by Basia Stryjecka on CreativeMarket.com.

ISBN 978-1-7770331-2-5 (Paperback)

Reflective Bible Journal

HEAR GOD'S VOICE
& FOLLOW HIS LEAD

TARYN NERGAARD

typewriter creative co.

you are loved

Contents

Introduction

I wish I could tell you that I created this journal just for you, but truthfully, I created it for myself first.

I've known for several years that the closeness I feel with God often corresponds to how much time I spend with him. More than that, it depends on my daily conversations with him—the active listening, the childlike questions, the adult doubts, and the humble posture.

I also know that I experience the most growth when I bring those conversations to life by applying what he has spoken to me and moving forward how he has directed me.

But somehow life creeps in and what felt important yesterday gets pushed aside by what feels urgent now. Maybe you can relate to how suddenly a day goes by and then a week and maybe even a month or more since you last had a good heart-to-heart with God. Then that closeness you once felt has slipped away and the ache of spiritual growth has changed to the pain of spiritual stagnation.

Those are the feelings I experienced recently and the reason I created this journal. I wanted to get back to a daily habit of abiding deeply in Christ.

This journal you hold in your hands is neither a promise nor a commandment. It holds no power to change your life. What it does contain is an invitation. It's an invitation to meet daily with God and to reflect weekly on how you're doing now and where you can continue to grow.

So, if you need more of Jesus—if your soul craves to be more surrendered to the life God is calling you to, then I hope this journal gently, but firmly, takes you by the hand and draws you nearer and deeper into the hope, joy, peace, and purpose that Jesus promises.

I'm with you.

- Taryn

Using the Journal

On the following pages you'll find recommendations for how I see this journal being used. I call these recommendations rather than instructions because I trust that God will lead you through your daily time with him. However, I believe this section to be important so I know that I'm helping you make the most out of this little journal and your investment in your spiritual formation.

In addition to this "Using the Journal" section, be sure to flip to the back of the journal to the "Resources" section for reading plans, prayers, lists of emotions, and more.

SEASONAL GROWTH PLAN

Have you ever failed to follow through with a resolution? Or have you ever set a goal for yourself and quit before you achieved it?

There are several reasons we fail to reach our goals or stick with our resolutions, but one of the simplest to fix is making sure our goals are important to us. We won't have the internal motivation to stick to our commitments unless we have a strong desire to make the goal a priority.

We need to have a strong connection to why we want something.

The following exercise is adapted from the program *Authentic Living* by Ken Dyck.[1] I have simplified it and adapted it to be a quarterly priority-planning exercise. In my own life, I need a reminder to assess my life and priorities regularly, and I find a greater sense of peace and freedom knowing that I can change this "plan" as my life changes throughout the year. There are three key components to the seasonal growth planning exercise:

1. Relational Priorities

This exercise prompts you to identify five relational priorities in your life. The first two have been filled in for you: God and Myself. The other three can include a spouse, children (grouped together or separately), friendships, extended family, etc.

Having our goals centered on relational priorities ensures that there is a deeper intrinsic motivation. It also helps keep our focus on relationships rather than material gains.

2. Relational Values

It's not enough to say that someone is a priority; we must identify why the relationship is a priority. To do that, we must consider and write down why we value each relationship. This is the step that solidifies our commitment to each relational priority.

3. Specific Actions

Vague goals are difficult to reach. Having specific, defined, and measurable action steps allows us to see our progress and define our success.

Consider these examples:

- I will spend more time with God.
- I will read my Bible for 5 minutes every day.

The first example is vague and difficult to measure, therefore difficult to put into practice. The second example is specific; it says exactly what the commitment is.

Setting specific goals gives us clear action steps for how we will make each relationship a priority. Here are two examples taken from a past seasonal growth plan I wrote for my own life:

I value GOD because he has done everything for me. Without him,

I am nothing.

- Therefore, I will make him a priority by starting my day in prayer and reading my Bible at least 5 days a week.
- I will write down what I hear God speak to me so that I will listen and obey to the best of my ability.
- I will trust God with my money by sticking to a budget.

I value MYSELF because God made me with a purpose, for a purpose.

- Therefore, I will eat food that I know gives my mind clarity and my body energy. Treats will be for enjoyment, not emotional fulfillment.
- I will exercise at least 3 times a week to strengthen my body.
- I will read daily to fill my mind with knowledge that helps me grow.

In recent seasons, I've been able to get even more specific about some of those action steps. Each season, you reevaluate and adjust the direction you want to go.

One of the greatest results of this exercise is seeing how much progress you make on your goals simply because you took the time to focus on what is important to you. When we center our minds on what we truly value, we naturally work towards those outcomes. You may not consciously be working on all 5 of these priorities at once, but your choices and decisions will shift in the right direction and begin to make progress throughout your life.

DAILY BIBLE READING

According to a study done by LifeWay research in 2017, almost nine out of ten American households own a Bible but more than half of Americans have read little or none of the Bible.[2]

If you fit into the 53% of people who have read less than half of the Bible, you likely haven't experienced the Bible as an intimate, active conversation with God.

If you have read through the Bible in the past but struggle to make it a meaningful part of your day, it's time to view the Bible as a method of life transformation through communication with God.

Information + Application = Transformation

Studying your Bible is important. It's good to know the context in which words are said and understand the meaning behind specific words and verses. But if the purpose of reading your Bible is to analyze the text without learning how to apply it to your life, then you're missing out on the opportunity for transformational life change.

Most of us don't plan on becoming theologians and biblical scholars, so why do we spend our reading time acting like knowledge is the ultimate goal?

When we begin a conversation with God through his Word, we gain a better understanding of our purpose, our direction, and our immediate next steps. He gives us the wisdom we need to honor him with our lives.

What You Need

To read God's word, you need a Bible. For this method, I recommend a physical Bible, but the YouVersion Bible app is a good second choice. Be sure to choose a translation you can understand.

Additionally, have this journal and a pen ready.

What to Read

Pick a book of the Bible and read through it in small portions each day (10-15 verses). It's better to read a small passage that you can remember and apply to your life than a large passage that overwhelms you with information.

Tip: If you're new to reading the Bible, start in the New Testament.

Write it Down

When we want to remember something important, we write it down. We should do the same thing when we spend time with God. Expect him to speak to you and value his words enough to remember them.

On your daily journal pages, write the date and reflect on how you are feeling at the moment. Be as specific as possible. If recognizing your emotions is difficult or new for you, see the resource section for help.

Next, follow the format as you go through the steps.

- Read
- Receive (no journal space for this prompt)
- Reflect
- Respond
- Remember

Read

Start reading. When something stands out to you, use your pen to place a mark in your Bible. Marking with a pen gives you more options than simply highlighting everything.

I use a small tick (`) to note something that stood out to me. For parts that really catch my attention, I use square brackets ([ ]) around the phrase. For single words that seem significant or are repeated, I use an underline (_).

Choose what works best for you. The purpose is to engage with what you are reading.

In your journal, write down the verse you read. You can also include a summary in your own words.

Receive

After you've written down the part of the passage that stood out to you, pray. Ask God what message or truth he wants to impress upon you with that Scripture.

Dig deeper by asking specific questions:

What do you want to teach me with this verse? How does this verse apply to my day today? Is there something you would like me to start doing? Is there something you would like me to stop doing?

Through this process, you are engaging in conversation with God regarding what he wants to talk to you about.

Reflect

Now take the time to write down what you feel God spoke to you. You don't need to worry about getting it exactly right! Just summarize the general message you felt he was trying to impress upon you.

If any other Bible verses come to your mind that relate to what you read, write them down in the margin to look up later.

In addition, take a moment to think of any action steps you can apply to your day or your life based on what you've just learned.

Respond

Now is the time to continue the conversation with God through prayer. Thank God for his faithfulness in your life, the truths he is teaching you, or anything else for which you feel grateful.

It's at this point in my own routine that I bring my wants, needs, and desires before God. By focusing on learning from him first and then bringing my needs to him second, I come before him with humility and openness.

Write your prayers in your journal as a way to recall past requests and remind yourself of his faithfulness.

Remember

Write out a verse to memorize this week. Writing it out will help you to remember it, and being able to recall Scripture is an important part of connecting your daily life to God's presence.

If you find Scripture memorization challenging, don't put pressure on yourself to memorize a new verse each week. Simply repeat the same verse until you're ready to move on.

The Holy Spirit

When Christ ascended to heaven, he promised his disciples that he would send them a helper. We understand this helper to be the Holy Spirit--an integral, but often overlooked, part of the Trinity.

When we engage in a conversation with God through the Holy Spirit, we are able to hear his Word speaking directly into our lives.

One of the greatest transformations of my life came as I learned to engage in my daily Bible reading this way.[3]

WEEKLY REFLECTION

This is an opportunity to recognize what is going well and where you need to make adjustments. Rather than allowing certain emotions or relational conflicts to build up, you can address them more frequently.

Personal Reflection

Be honest and allow yourself to celebrate the highs and make space for the lows. We cannot grow from a place of shame, so it's best to "make friends" with all the parts of ourselves, even the ones we'd like to change.

Relational Reflection

If you're not used to dealing with conflict or you live in a constant state of shame or bitterness, this section might feel unbearable at first. But take heart—as we learn to make this a regular part of our lives, it becomes a practice that changes us from the inside out. It is worth the discomfort.

First, think of any hurts you feel from this week (or if some of them have lingered there longer, address these too). When our hurt is left unaddressed, it becomes bitterness—a self-inflicted poison of our souls.

Use the Prayer of Forgiveness in the Resources section or pray your own prayer of forgiveness to release the hurt and bitterness. Even if you think something *isn't a big deal*, it's best to forgive the person now. Relational molehills do become mountains when we ignore them too long.

Next, identify anyone you may have hurt this week. Use the Prayer of Repentance to admit your wrongdoing to God, then make things right with the person you hurt (see Resources section for helpful information).

We live in a lonely culture, yet we're often waiting for others to go first in initiating friendships. Make the decision to connect with someone in person or through a phone call or text each week.

Spiritual Reflection

This section of your weekly reflection helps pull together your daily time with God. Look back through your "Reflect" writing from each day and identify any similar impressions you felt God spoke to you.

Has God been affirming similar ideas or truths to you through other sources? This is the place to make those connections and recognize all the ways God is speaking to you regularly.

After your week of spending daily time with God, are there any questions you have for him? Don't be afraid to search your heart and mind for areas of doubt you are facing. God can handle our questions and doubts—it does not mean we lack faith!

Coming before God with an open and honest heart is what he desires.

Next Week

It's important to have something to look forward to. It can be anything of any size—as long as it brings you joy! If you can't think of anything you are looking forward to, plan something now.

Additionally, this is your space to decide a verse to memorize next week. Again, don't push yourself to move on to a new verse if you're still learning the one from this week. Keep going with the same one until you're comfortable with it. This isn't a race or a competition, so go as slow and steady as you need.

You can see a sample of my own use of the journal on the following pages. Some days you'll fill the whole space, other times you might only write a of couple words.

Date: January 1, 2020

Today, I feel: isolated & disappointed

READ

Today, I read: Philippians 1:1-14

What stood out to me is:

Verse 6... "he who began a good work in you will carry it out to completion..."

REFLECT

What I best sense God speaking to me is:

He is faithful. I don't need to know all the answers or see what's coming in the future—I can trust that God is working out the details. Have faith!

The one thing I will surrender to God today is:

Whether or not I get the job.

One next step I can take today is:

Plan my budget for this month.

RESPOND

God, thank you for reminding me not to worry because you're in control. Help me trust you when I'm feeling overwhelmed and anxious. Please show what is important to focus on today and help me let go of everything else. Be with me today as I parent and work—give me patience and love for everyone I'm around today. Thank you God. Amen.

REMEMBER

Romans 8:5-6

For those who live according to the flesh have their minds set on the things of the flesh, but those who live according to the Spirit have their minds set on the things of the Spirit. Now the mind-set of the flesh is death, but the mind-set of the Spirit is life and peace.

Weekly Reflection

PERSONAL REFLECTION

What went well this week?

> We had a relaxing time over the holidays as a family. I didn't get anxious about things that weren't important.

Three things I am grateful for are:

> 1. Our little family
>
> 2. Meaningful work
>
> 3. Our church

What feeling(s) did I experience most frequently? Why?

> Isolated, lonely. The holidays remind me that people around me don't know me very well. It would be nice to feel truly seen and known.

What thoughts or worries came to mind most frequently?

That I may never really fit in or be included.

RELATIONAL REFLECTION

Who do I need to forgive?

Jessica

With whom do I need to make things right?

Becca

I will do that by:

Apologizing for not texting her over the holidays and inviting her for coffee.

One person I will connect with next week is:

Becca

SPIRITUAL REFLECTION

Is there a theme God has been speaking to me about this week through Bible reading, worship, books, or sermons?

That everyone feels rejection. I should still choose to connect with people and not feel hurt when relationships aren't reciprocated.

The questions I have for God right now are:

Why are relationships so hard?? How can I be a better wife and a better friend?

NEXT WEEK

I am looking forward to...

My kid-free day!

Next week's memory verse:

Romans 8:37-39

Seasonal Growth Plan

Seasonal Growth Plan

This growth plan is for the months of: ....

I will reevaluate this plan on: ....

As best I understand today, my sense of purpose, ministry, and calling from God is:

My verse for this season is:

I value GOD because...

Therefore, I will...

I will...

I value MYSELF because...

Therefore, I will...

I will...

I value.................................... because...

Therefore, I will...

I will...

I value.................................... because...

Therefore, I will...

I will...

I value .... because...

Therefore, I will...

I will...

Journal

Week of

....

For freedom, Christ set us free. Stand firm then
and don't submit again to a yoke of slavery.

Galatians 5:1

Notes

Date:

Today, I feel: ....

READ

Today, I read: ....

What stood out to me is:

REFLECT

What I best sense God speaking to me is:

The one thing I will surrender to God today is:

One next step I can take today is:

RESPOND

REMEMBER

Date:

Today, I feel: ....

READ

Today, I read: ....

What stood out to me is:

REFLECT

What I best sense God speaking to me is:

The one thing I will surrender to God today is:

One next step I can take today is:

RESPOND

REMEMBER

Date:

Today, I feel:

READ

Today, I read:

What stood out to me is:

REFLECT

What I best sense God speaking to me is:

The one thing I will surrender to God today is:

One next step I can take today is:

RESPOND

REMEMBER

Date:

Today, I feel:

READ

Today, I read:

What stood out to me is:

REFLECT

What I best sense God speaking to me is:

The one thing I will surrender to God today is:

One next step I can take today is:

RESPOND

REMEMBER

Date:

Today, I feel:

READ

Today, I read:

What stood out to me is:

REFLECT

What I best sense God speaking to me is:

The one thing I will surrender to God today is:

One next step I can take today is:

RESPOND

REMEMBER

Weekly Reflection

PERSONAL REFLECTION

What went well this week?

Three things I am grateful for are:

1.

2.

3.

What feeling(s) did I experience most frequently? Why?

What thoughts or worries came to mind most frequently?

RELATIONAL REFLECTION

Who do I need to forgive?

With whom do I need to make things right?

I will do that by:

One person I will connect with next week is:

SPIRITUAL REFLECTION

Is there a theme God has been speaking to me about this week through Bible reading, worship, books, or sermons?

The questions I have for God right now are:

NEXT WEEK

I am looking forward to...

Next week's memory verse:

Week of

. . . .

I called to the Lord in distress; the Lord answered
me and put me in a spacious place.

Psalm 118:5

Notes

Date:

Today, I feel:

READ

Today, I read:

What stood out to me is:

REFLECT

What I best sense God speaking to me is:

The one thing I will surrender to God today is:

One next step I can take today is:

RESPOND

REMEMBER

59

Date:

Today, I feel:

READ

Today, I read:

What stood out to me is:

REFLECT

What I best sense God speaking to me is:

The one thing I will surrender to God today is:

One next step I can take today is:

RESPOND

REMEMBER

Date:

Today, I feel:

READ

Today, I read:

What stood out to me is:

REFLECT

What I best sense God speaking to me is:

The one thing I will surrender to God today is:

One next step I can take today is:

RESPOND

REMEMBER

Date:

Today, I feel:

READ

Today, I read:

What stood out to me is:

REFLECT

What I best sense God speaking to me is:

The one thing I will surrender to God today is:

One next step I can take today is:

RESPOND

REMEMBER

Date:

Today, I feel:

READ

Today, I read:

What stood out to me is:

REFLECT

What I best sense God speaking to me is:

The one thing I will surrender to God today is:

One next step I can take today is:

RESPOND

REMEMBER

Weekly Reflection

PERSONAL REFLECTION

What went well this week?

Three things I am grateful for are:

1.

2.

3.

What feeling(s) did I experience most frequently? Why?

What thoughts or worries came to mind most frequently?

RELATIONAL REFLECTION

Who do I need to forgive?

With whom do I need to make things right?

I will do that by:

One person I will connect with next week is:

SPIRITUAL REFLECTION

Is there a theme God has been speaking to me about this week through Bible reading, worship, books, or sermons?

The questions I have for God right now are:

NEXT WEEK

I am looking forward to...

Next week's memory verse:

Week of

....

Jesus spoke to them again: "I am the light of the
world. Anyone who follows me will never walk in
the darkness but will have the light of life."

John 8:12

Notes

Date:

Today, I feel:

READ

Today, I read:

What stood out to me is:

REFLECT

What I best sense God speaking to me is:

The one thing I will surrender to God today is:

One next step I can take today is:

RESPOND

REMEMBER

Date:

Today, I feel:

READ

Today, I read:

What stood out to me is:

REFLECT

What I best sense God speaking to me is:

The one thing I will surrender to God today is:

One next step I can take today is:

RESPOND

REMEMBER

Date:

Today, I feel:

READ

Today, I read:

What stood out to me is:

REFLECT

What I best sense God speaking to me is:

The one thing I will surrender to God today is:

One next step I can take today is:

RESPOND

REMEMBER

Date:

Today, I feel:

READ

Today, I read:

What stood out to me is:

REFLECT

What I best sense God speaking to me is:

The one thing I will surrender to God today is:

One next step I can take today is:

RESPOND

REMEMBER

Date:

Today, I feel:

READ

Today, I read:

What stood out to me is:

REFLECT

What I best sense God speaking to me is:

The one thing I will surrender to God today is:

One next step I can take today is:

RESPOND

REMEMBER

Weekly Reflection

PERSONAL REFLECTION

What went well this week?

Three things I am grateful for are:

1.

2.

3.

What feeling(s) did I experience most frequently? Why?

What thoughts or worries came to mind most frequently?

RELATIONAL REFLECTION

Who do I need to forgive?

With whom do I need to make things right?

I will do that by:

One person I will connect with next week is:

SPIRITUAL REFLECTION

Is there a theme God has been speaking to me about this week through Bible reading, worship, books, or sermons?

The questions I have for God right now are:

NEXT WEEK

I am looking forward to...

Next week's memory verse:

Week of

....

Now the Lord is the Spirit, and where the
Spirit of the Lord is, there is freedom.

2 Corinthians 3:17

Notes

Date:

Today, I feel:

READ

Today, I read:

What stood out to me is:

REFLECT

What I best sense God speaking to me is:

The one thing I will surrender to God today is:

One next step I can take today is:

RESPOND

REMEMBER

Date:

Today, I feel:

READ

Today, I read:

What stood out to me is:

REFLECT

What I best sense God speaking to me is:

The one thing I will surrender to God today is:

One next step I can take today is:

RESPOND

REMEMBER

Date:

Today, I feel:

READ

Today, I read:

What stood out to me is:

REFLECT

What I best sense God speaking to me is:

The one thing I will surrender to God today is:

One next step I can take today is:

RESPOND

REMEMBER

105

Date:

Today, I feel: ....

READ

Today, I read: ....

What stood out to me is:

REFLECT

What I best sense God speaking to me is:

The one thing I will surrender to God today is:

One next step I can take today is:

RESPOND

REMEMBER

Date:

Today, I feel:

READ

Today, I read:

What stood out to me is:

REFLECT

What I best sense God speaking to me is:

The one thing I will surrender to God today is:

One next step I can take today is:

RESPOND

REMEMBER

Weekly Reflection

PERSONAL REFLECTION

What went well this week?

Three things I am grateful for are:

1.

2.

3.

What feeling(s) did I experience most frequently? Why?

What thoughts or worries came to mind most frequently?

RELATIONAL REFLECTION

Who do I need to forgive?

With whom do I need to make things right?

I will do that by:

One person I will connect with next week is:

SPIRITUAL REFLECTION

Is there a theme God has been speaking to me about this week through Bible reading, worship, books, or sermons?

The questions I have for God right now are:

NEXT WEEK

I am looking forward to...

Next week's memory verse:

Week of

....

This is my comfort in my affliction: Your
promise has given me life.

Psalm 119:50

Notes

Date:

Today, I feel:

READ

Today, I read:

What stood out to me is:

REFLECT

What I best sense God speaking to me is:

The one thing I will surrender to God today is:

One next step I can take today is:

RESPOND

REMEMBER

Date:

Today, I feel:

READ

Today, I read:

What stood out to me is:

REFLECT

What I best sense God speaking to me is:

The one thing I will surrender to God today is:

One next step I can take today is:

RESPOND

REMEMBER

Date:

Today, I feel: ....

READ

Today, I read: ....

What stood out to me is:

REFLECT

What I best sense God speaking to me is:

The one thing I will surrender to God today is:

One next step I can take today is:

RESPOND

REMEMBER

Date:

Today, I feel:

READ

Today, I read:

What stood out to me is:

REFLECT

What I best sense God speaking to me is:

The one thing I will surrender to God today is:

One next step I can take today is:

RESPOND

REMEMBER

Date:

Today, I feel:

READ

Today, I read:

What stood out to me is:

REFLECT

What I best sense God speaking to me is:

The one thing I will surrender to God today is:

One next step I can take today is:

RESPOND

REMEMBER

Weekly Reflection

PERSONAL REFLECTION

What went well this week?

Three things I am grateful for are:

1.

2.

3.

What feeling(s) did I experience most frequently? Why?

What thoughts or worries came to mind most frequently?

RELATIONAL REFLECTION

Who do I need to forgive?

With whom do I need to make things right?

I will do that by:

One person I will connect with next week is:

SPIRITUAL REFLECTION

Is there a theme God has been speaking to me about this week through Bible reading, worship, books, or sermons?

The questions I have for God right now are:

NEXT WEEK

I am looking forward to...

Next week's memory verse:

Week of

....

For you were called to be free, brothers and sisters;
only don't use this freedom as an opportunity for
the flesh, but serve one another through love.

Galatians 5:13

Notes

Date:

Today, I feel:

READ

Today, I read:

What stood out to me is:

REFLECT

What I best sense God speaking to me is:

The one thing I will surrender to God today is:

One next step I can take today is:

RESPOND

REMEMBER

Date:

Today, I feel: ....

READ

Today, I read: ....

What stood out to me is:

REFLECT

What I best sense God speaking to me is:

The one thing I will surrender to God today is:

One next step I can take today is:

RESPOND

REMEMBER

Date:

Today, I feel:

READ

Today, I read:

What stood out to me is:

REFLECT

What I best sense God speaking to me is:

The one thing I will surrender to God today is:

One next step I can take today is:

RESPOND

REMEMBER

Date:

Today, I feel: ....

READ

Today, I read: ....

What stood out to me is:

REFLECT

What I best sense God speaking to me is:

The one thing I will surrender to God today is:

One next step I can take today is:

RESPOND

REMEMBER

Date:

Today, I feel: ....

READ

Today, I read: ....

What stood out to me is:

REFLECT

What I best sense God speaking to me is:

The one thing I will surrender to God today is:

One next step I can take today is:

RESPOND

REMEMBER

Weekly Reflection

PERSONAL REFLECTION

What went well this week?

Three things I am grateful for are:

1.

2.

3.

What feeling(s) did I experience most frequently? Why?

What thoughts or worries came to mind most frequently?

RELATIONAL REFLECTION

Who do I need to forgive?

With whom do I need to make things right?

I will do that by:

One person I will connect with next week is:

SPIRITUAL REFLECTION

Is there a theme God has been speaking to me about this week through Bible reading, worship, books, or sermons?

The questions I have for God right now are:

NEXT WEEK

I am looking forward to...

Next week's memory verse:

Week of

. . . .

But now, since you have been set free from sin and have become enslaved to God, you have your fruit, which results in sanctification—and the outcome is eternal life!

Romans 6:22

Notes

Date:

Today, I feel:

READ

Today, I read:

What stood out to me is:

REFLECT

What I best sense God speaking to me is:

The one thing I will surrender to God today is:

One next step I can take today is:

RESPOND

REMEMBER

Date:

Today, I feel:

READ

Today, I read:

What stood out to me is:

REFLECT

What I best sense God speaking to me is:

The one thing I will surrender to God today is:

One next step I can take today is:

RESPOND

REMEMBER

Date:

Today, I feel:

READ

Today, I read:

What stood out to me is:

REFLECT

What I best sense God speaking to me is:

The one thing I will surrender to God today is:

One next step I can take today is:

RESPOND

REMEMBER

Date:

Today, I feel:

READ

Today, I read:

What stood out to me is:

REFLECT

What I best sense God speaking to me is:

The one thing I will surrender to God today is:

One next step I can take today is:

RESPOND

REMEMBER

Date:

Today, I feel:

READ

Today, I read:

What stood out to me is:

REFLECT

What I best sense God speaking to me is:

The one thing I will surrender to God today is:

One next step I can take today is:

RESPOND

REMEMBER

Weekly Reflection

PERSONAL REFLECTION

What went well this week?

Three things I am grateful for are:

1.

2.

3.

What feeling(s) did I experience most frequently? Why?

What thoughts or worries came to mind most frequently?

RELATIONAL REFLECTION

Who do I need to forgive?

With whom do I need to make things right?

I will do that by:

One person I will connect with next week is:

SPIRITUAL REFLECTION

Is there a theme God has been speaking to me about this week through Bible reading, worship, books, or sermons?

The questions I have for God right now are:

NEXT WEEK

I am looking forward to...

Next week's memory verse:

Week of

....

So if the Son sets you free, you really will be free.

John 8:36

Notes

Date:

Today, I feel: ....

READ

Today, I read: ....

What stood out to me is:

REFLECT

What I best sense God speaking to me is:

The one thing I will surrender to God today is:

One next step I can take today is:

RESPOND

REMEMBER

Date:

Today, I feel: ....

READ

Today, I read: ....

What stood out to me is:

REFLECT

What I best sense God speaking to me is:

The one thing I will surrender to God today is:

One next step I can take today is:

RESPOND

REMEMBER

Date:

Today, I feel:

READ

Today, I read:

What stood out to me is:

REFLECT

What I best sense God speaking to me is:

The one thing I will surrender to God today is:

One next step I can take today is:

RESPOND

REMEMBER

Date:
....

Today, I feel: ....

READ

Today, I read: ....

What stood out to me is:

REFLECT

What I best sense God speaking to me is:

The one thing I will surrender to God today is:

One next step I can take today is:

RESPOND

REMEMBER

Date:

Today, I feel:

READ

Today, I read:

What stood out to me is:

REFLECT

What I best sense God speaking to me is:

The one thing I will surrender to God today is:

One next step I can take today is:

RESPOND

REMEMBER

Weekly Reflection

PERSONAL REFLECTION

What went well this week?

Three things I am grateful for are:

1.

2.

3.

What feeling(s) did I experience most frequently? Why?

What thoughts or worries came to mind most frequently?

RELATIONAL REFLECTION

Who do I need to forgive?

With whom do I need to make things right?

I will do that by:

One person I will connect with next week is:

SPIRITUAL REFLECTION

Is there a theme God has been speaking to me about this week through Bible reading, worship, books, or sermons?

The questions I have for God right now are:

NEXT WEEK

I am looking forward to...

Next week's memory verse:

Week of

. . . .

For as the earth produces its growth, and as a garden enables
what is sown to spring up, so the Lord God will cause
righteousness and praise to spring up before all the nations.

Isaiah 61:11

Notes

Date:

Today, I feel:

READ

Today, I read:

What stood out to me is:

REFLECT

What I best sense God speaking to me is:

The one thing I will surrender to God today is:

One next step I can take today is:

RESPOND

REMEMBER

Date:

Today, I feel:

READ

Today, I read:

What stood out to me is:

REFLECT

What I best sense God speaking to me is:

The one thing I will surrender to God today is:

One next step I can take today is:

RESPOND

REMEMBER

Date:

Today, I feel: ....

READ

Today, I read: ....

What stood out to me is:

REFLECT

What I best sense God speaking to me is:

The one thing I will surrender to God today is:

One next step I can take today is:

RESPOND

REMEMBER

Date:

Today, I feel:

READ

Today, I read:

What stood out to me is:

REFLECT

What I best sense God speaking to me is:

The one thing I will surrender to God today is:

One next step I can take today is:

RESPOND

REMEMBER

Date:

Today, I feel:

READ

Today, I read:

What stood out to me is:

REFLECT

What I best sense God speaking to me is:

The one thing I will surrender to God today is:

One next step I can take today is:

RESPOND

REMEMBER

Weekly Reflection

PERSONAL REFLECTION

What went well this week?

Three things I am grateful for are:

1.

2.

3.

What feeling(s) did I experience most frequently? Why?

What thoughts or worries came to mind most frequently?

RELATIONAL REFLECTION

Who do I need to forgive?

With whom do I need to make things right?

I will do that by:

One person I will connect with next week is:

SPIRITUAL REFLECTION

Is there a theme God has been speaking to me about this week through Bible reading, worship, books, or sermons?

The questions I have for God right now are:

NEXT WEEK

I am looking forward to...

Next week's memory verse:

Week of

....

Now those who belong to Christ Jesus have crucified
the flesh with its passions and desires.

Galatians 5:24

Notes

Date:

Today, I feel: ....

READ

Today, I read: ....

What stood out to me is:

REFLECT

What I best sense God speaking to me is:

The one thing I will surrender to God today is:

One next step I can take today is:

RESPOND

REMEMBER

Date:

Today, I feel:

READ

Today, I read:

What stood out to me is:

REFLECT

What I best sense God speaking to me is:

The one thing I will surrender to God today is:

One next step I can take today is:

RESPOND

REMEMBER

Date:

Today, I feel:

READ

Today, I read:

What stood out to me is:

REFLECT

What I best sense God speaking to me is:

The one thing I will surrender to God today is:

One next step I can take today is:

RESPOND

REMEMBER

Date:

Today, I feel:

READ

Today, I read:

What stood out to me is:

REFLECT

What I best sense God speaking to me is:

The one thing I will surrender to God today is:

One next step I can take today is:

RESPOND

REMEMBER

Date:

Today, I feel:

READ

Today, I read:

What stood out to me is:

REFLECT

What I best sense God speaking to me is:

The one thing I will surrender to God today is:

One next step I can take today is:

RESPOND

REMEMBER

Weekly Reflection

PERSONAL REFLECTION

What went well this week?

Three things I am grateful for are:

1.

2.

3.

What feeling(s) did I experience most frequently? Why?

What thoughts or worries came to mind most frequently?

RELATIONAL REFLECTION

Who do I need to forgive?

With whom do I need to make things right?

I will do that by:

One person I will connect with next week is:

SPIRITUAL REFLECTION

Is there a theme God has been speaking to me about this week through Bible reading, worship, books, or sermons?

The questions I have for God right now are:

NEXT WEEK

I am looking forward to...

Next week's memory verse:

Week of

....

"Everything is permissible for me," but not everything
is beneficial. "Everything is permissible for me,"
but I will not be mastered by anything.

1 Corinthians 6:12

Notes

Date:

Today, I feel:

READ

Today, I read:

What stood out to me is:

REFLECT

What I best sense God speaking to me is:

The one thing I will surrender to God today is:

One next step I can take today is:

RESPOND

REMEMBER

Date:

Today, I feel:

READ

Today, I read:

What stood out to me is:

REFLECT

What I best sense God speaking to me is:

The one thing I will surrender to God today is:

One next step I can take today is:

RESPOND

REMEMBER

Date:

Today, I feel:

READ

Today, I read:

What stood out to me is:

REFLECT

What I best sense God speaking to me is:

The one thing I will surrender to God today is:

One next step I can take today is:

RESPOND

REMEMBER

Date:

Today, I feel:

READ

Today, I read:

What stood out to me is:

REFLECT

What I best sense God speaking to me is:

The one thing I will surrender to God today is:

One next step I can take today is:

RESPOND

REMEMBER

Date:

Today, I feel: ....

READ

Today, I read: ....

What stood out to me is:

REFLECT

What I best sense God speaking to me is:

The one thing I will surrender to God today is:

One next step I can take today is:

RESPOND

REMEMBER

Weekly Reflection

PERSONAL REFLECTION

What went well this week?

Three things I am grateful for are:

1.

2.

3.

What feeling(s) did I experience most frequently? Why?

What thoughts or worries came to mind most frequently?

RELATIONAL REFLECTION

Who do I need to forgive?

With whom do I need to make things right?

I will do that by:

One person I will connect with next week is:

SPIRITUAL REFLECTION

Is there a theme God has been speaking to me about this week through Bible reading, worship, books, or sermons?

The questions I have for God right now are:

NEXT WEEK

I am looking forward to...

Next week's memory verse:

Week of

. . . .

Then Jesus said to the Jews who had believed him, "If you continue in my word, you really are my disciples. You will know the truth, and the truth will set you free."

John 8:31-32

Notes

Date:

Today, I feel: ....

READ

Today, I read: ....

What stood out to me is:

REFLECT

What I best sense God speaking to me is:

The one thing I will surrender to God today is:

One next step I can take today is:

RESPOND

REMEMBER

Date:

Today, I feel:

READ

Today, I read:

What stood out to me is:

REFLECT

What I best sense God speaking to me is:

The one thing I will surrender to God today is:

One next step I can take today is:

RESPOND

REMEMBER

Date:

Today, I feel:

READ

Today, I read:

What stood out to me is:

REFLECT

What I best sense God speaking to me is:

The one thing I will surrender to God today is:

One next step I can take today is:

RESPOND

REMEMBER

Date:

Today, I feel:

READ

Today, I read:

What stood out to me is:

REFLECT

What I best sense God speaking to me is:

The one thing I will surrender to God today is:

One next step I can take today is:

RESPOND

REMEMBER

Date:

Today, I feel:

READ

Today, I read:

What stood out to me is:

REFLECT

What I best sense God speaking to me is:

The one thing I will surrender to God today is:

One next step I can take today is:

RESPOND

REMEMBER

Weekly Reflection

PERSONAL REFLECTION

What went well this week?

Three things I am grateful for are:

1.

2.

3.

What feeling(s) did I experience most frequently? Why?

What thoughts or worries came to mind most frequently?

RELATIONAL REFLECTION

Who do I need to forgive?

With whom do I need to make things right?

I will do that by:

One person I will connect with next week is:

SPIRITUAL REFLECTION

Is there a theme God has been speaking to me about this week through Bible reading, worship, books, or sermons?

The questions I have for God right now are:

NEXT WEEK

I am looking forward to...

Next week's memory verse:

Week of

....

Do not be conformed to this age, but be transformed
by the renewing of your mind, so that you may discern
what is the good, pleasing, and perfect will of God.

Romans 12:2

Notes

Date:

Today, I feel: ....

READ

Today, I read: ....

What stood out to me is:

REFLECT

What I best sense God speaking to me is:

The one thing I will surrender to God today is:

One next step I can take today is:

RESPOND

REMEMBER

Date:

Today, I feel:

READ

Today, I read:

What stood out to me is:

REFLECT

What I best sense God speaking to me is:

The one thing I will surrender to God today is:

One next step I can take today is:

RESPOND

REMEMBER

Date:

Today, I feel:

READ

Today, I read:

What stood out to me is:

REFLECT

What I best sense God speaking to me is:

The one thing I will surrender to God today is:

One next step I can take today is:

RESPOND

REMEMBER

Date:

Today, I feel: ....

READ

Today, I read: ....

What stood out to me is:

REFLECT

What I best sense God speaking to me is:

The one thing I will surrender to God today is:

One next step I can take today is:

RESPOND

REMEMBER

Date:

Today, I feel: ....

READ

Today, I read: ....

What stood out to me is:

REFLECT

What I best sense God speaking to me is:

The one thing I will surrender to God today is:

One next step I can take today is:

RESPOND

REMEMBER

Weekly Reflection

PERSONAL REFLECTION

What went well this week?

Three things I am grateful for are:

1.

2.

3.

What feeling(s) did I experience most frequently? Why?

What thoughts or worries came to mind most frequently?

RELATIONAL REFLECTION

Who do I need to forgive?

With whom do I need to make things right?

I will do that by:

One person I will connect with next week is:

SPIRITUAL REFLECTION

Is there a theme God has been speaking to me about this week through Bible reading, worship, books, or sermons?

The questions I have for God right now are:

NEXT WEEK

I am looking forward to...

Next week's memory verse:

Seasonal Reflection

Looking back & forward...

Congratulations on completing the *Reflective Bible Journal!*

Whether it took you 13 weeks or 52 weeks, I celebrate your commitment to meeting with God regularly.

Let's take a quick look back at your journey...

A highlight from my time with God is:

The progress I made on my *Seasonal Growth Plan* is:

Growth I experienced in my personal development is:

Growth I experienced in my spiritual development is:

Growth I experienced in my relational development is:

> *(blank box)*

Let's look forward...

One thing I want to continue moving forward is:

> *(blank box)*

One thing I want to change moving forward is:

> *(blank box)*

I am grateful for:

1.

2.

3.

4.

5.

Resources

65-Day Reading Plan

DAY	VERSES	DAY	VERSES
1	Galatians 1:1-10	18	Ephesians 2:11-22
2	Galatians 1:11-24	19	Ephesians 3:1-13
3	Galatians 2:1-10	20	Ephesians 3:14-21
4	Galatians 2:11-21	21	Ephesians 4:1-16
5	Galatians 3:1-9	22	Ephesians 4:17-32
6	Galatians 3:10-18	23	Ephesians 5:1-7
7	Galatians 3:19-29	24	Ephesians 5:8-20
8	Galatians 4:1-7	25	Ephesians 5:21-33
9	Galatians 4:8-20	26	Ephesians 6:1-9
10	Galatians 4:21-31	27	Ephesians 6:10-24
11	Galatians 5:1-12	28	James 1:1-8
12	Galatians 5:13-26	29	James 1:9-11
13	Galatians 6:1-10	30	James 1:12-18
14	Galatians 6:11-18	31	James 1:19-21
15	Ephesians 1:1-14	32	James 1:22-27
16	Ephesians 1:15-23	33	James 2:1-7
17	Ephesians 2:1-10	34	James 2:8-13

DAY	VERSES	DAY	VERSES
35	James 2:14-19	51	1 Peter 1:17-25
36	James 2:20-26	52	1 Peter 2:1-10
37	James 3:1-6	53	1 Peter 2:11-25
38	James 3:7-12	54	1 Peter 3:1-7
39	James 3:13-16	55	1 Peter 3:8-22
40	James 3:17-18	56	1 Peter 4:1-11
41	James 4:1-6	57	1 Peter 4:12-19
42	James 4:7-10	58	1 Peter 5:1-7
43	James 4:11-12	59	1 Peter 5:8-14
44	James 4:13-17	60	2 Peter 1:1-11
45	James 5:1-6	61	2 Peter 1:12-21
46	James 5:7-12	62	2 Peter 2:1-9
47	James 5:13-16	63	2 Peter 2:10-22
48	James 5:17-20	64	2 Peter 3:1-9
49	1 Peter 1:1-9	65	2 Peter 3:10-18
50	1 Peter 1:10-16		

For more reading plan suggestions, visit
tarynnergaard.com/readingplans.

Emotions

Try to narrow down your emotions and be specifc about how you are feeling.

Choose the initial emotion you feel (happy, fearful, disgusted, sad, angry, bad, surprised) and work towards the column on the far right.[4]

HAPPY		
	Content	Free / Joyful
	Interested	Curious / Inquisitive
	Proud	Successful / Confident
	Accepted	Respected / Valued
	Powerful	Courageous / Creative
	Peaceful	Loving / Thankful
	Trusting	Sensitive / Intimate
	Optimistic	Hopeful / Inspired

FEARFUL	Scared	Helpless
		Frightened
	Anxious	Overwhelmed
		Worried
	Insecure	Inadequate
		Inferior
	Weak	Worthless
		Insignificant
	Rejected	Excluded
		Persecuted
	Threatened	Nervous
		Exposed

DISGUSTED	Disapproving	Judgmental
		Embarrassed
	Disappointed	Appalled
		Revolted
	Awful	Nauseated
		Detestable
	Repelled	Horrified
		Hesitant

SURPRISED	Startled	Shocked
		Dismayed
	Confused	Disillusioned
		Perplexed
	Amazed	Astonished
		Awed
	Excited	Eager
		Energetic

ANGRY	Let down	Betrayed Resentful
	Humiliated	Disrespected Ridiculed
	Bitter	Indignant Violated
	Mad	Furious Jealous
	Aggressive	Provoked Hostile
	Frustrated	Infuriated Annoyed
	Distant	Withdrawn Numb
	Critical	Skeptical Dismissive

BAD	Bored	Indifferent Apathetic
	Busy	Pressured Rushed
	Stressed	Overwhelmed Out of control
	Tired	Sleepy Unfocused

S A D	Lonely	Isolated Abandoned
	Vulnerable	Victimised Fragile
	Despairing	Grieving Powerless
	Guilty	Ashamed Remorseful
	Depressed	Inferior Empty
	Hurt	Embarrassed Disappointed

Prayer of Forgiveness

God, I choose to forgive [name]. When he/she [words or situation that caused hurt], it made me feel [emotions and pain].

As I have accepted your forgiveness for my own sins and shortcomings, I offer this forgiveness to [name]. Whether or not he/she deserves my forgiveness and whether he/she asks for forgiveness, I will freely give it because of your death on the cross.

When I see [name] again, help me recall this prayer and hold captive any thoughts towards him/her that are not merciful and filled with grace. Help me to see him/her the way you do and help me to love him/her as you do.

I pray that [name] would receive your forgiveness and your blessing. I release him/her to your care and choose to no longer carry this burden of bitterness. Please heal my heart and help me not to allow this hurt to distance myself from others. Thank you for your extravagant love.

Amen.

Prayer of Repentance

God, forgive me for [words or actions]. My words/actions caused [result of words or actions]. Above all, I know my sin is separating me from your intimate presence. I am sorry, God.

Please help me release the shame and regret I feel, knowing that I am undeserving of your extravagant love and endless grace, yet you give them to me freely. I forgive myself and let go of all self-hatred and condemnation.

Allow your conviction to continue to bring me towards you in repentance instead of hiding my sin. Shine your light of truth in any other area of my heart that I need to repent of now.

[Pause for reflection and repeat the first paragraph for any other areas of sin God brings to mind.]

Thank you for your forgiveness. Help me resist the temptation to repeat my sin or punish myself for my past sins. I accept your forgiveness and move forward in love and grace.

Amen.

Making Amends

WHAT DOES IT MEAN TO MAKE AMENDS?

Making amends means to do something to correct a mistake that one has made or a bad situation that one has caused.[5]

It involves 3 parts:

- Sincere apology
- Change of behavior
- Restitution

APOLOGY

Your apology should be made in person or in writing. It should be specific about what you did that hurt them and the consequences that resulted. This is not a time to discuss what the other person may have done to hurt you—you are taking responsibility for your own actions, not pointing fingers or passing blame. Additionally, it is not your responsibility to encourage their forgiveness, nor is it your right to receive their forgiveness, so do not ask the other person to forgive you.

CHANGE OF BEHAVIOR

An apology without a change in behavior is worthless. Your actions speak louder than your words. True repentance is displayed when we turn away from our sin and act in the opposite spirit.

RESTITUTION

Beyond an apology and change of behavior, restitution needs to be made. This may mean returning what you stole, fixing what you broke, or paying for something to be replaced. This may be easier to see how it applies to tangible objects, but the same applies for people. It's much more difficult to heal a person than to fix a car, but do what you can to make up for the damage you caused.

DIRECT AND INDIRECT AMENDS

From the *12 Steps of Freedom Session*[6]: "We made specific and direct amends to those we have hurt whenever possible, except when to do so would further injure them or others who are innocent. For such persons, we made specific and indirect amends."

There are times when it is unwise or impossible to make a direct amends to the person you hurt.

An indirect amends should be made if a direct amends would cause serious, additional harm to the person you hurt. If you're considering an indirect amends, ask yourself: "Am I avoiding this conversation to protect myself or him/her?" This is also a good time to find someone you trust to confess this situation and ask for an objective opinion on whether you should directly or indirectly make amends.

If the person you hurt is no longer alive or they are unreachable, you should still make amends indirectly. Consider writing a letter of apology and discarding it and/or make a donation or serve an organization that would honor the person.

For additional resources visit
tarynnergaard.com/resources.

Notes

1. Dyck, Ken. Authentic Living. Freedom Session International, https://freedomsession.com/about/authentic-living/ Accessed 22 August 2020.

2. Smietana, Bob. "LifeWay Research: Americans Are Fond of the Bible, Don't Actually Read It." LifeWay Research, LifeWay Research, 25 April 2017, https://lifewayresearch.com/2017/04/25/lifeway-research-americans-are-fond-of-the-Bible-dont-actually-read-it. Accessed 7 January 2020.

3. I will be forever grateful to Ken Dyck, creator of Freedom Session, for his teaching on Bible reading.

4. These emotions were orginally published as an emotion wheel. Schuster, Sarah. "The 'Emotion Chart' My Therapist Gave Me That I Didn't Know I Needed." Yahoo!Lifestyle, Yahoo.com, 28 November 2018, https://www.yahoo.com/lifestyle/apos-emotion-chart-apos-therapist-002028240.html. Accessed 7 January 2020.

5. "Make amends." The Merriam-Webster.com Dictionary, Merriam-Webster Inc., https://www.merriam-webster.com/dictionary/make%20amends. Accessed 6 January 2020.

6. Dyck, Ken. "12 Steps of Freedom Session." Freedom Session, Freedom Session International, https://freedomsession.com/12-steps-of-freedom-session. Accessed 6 January 2020.

Acknowledgments

This journal you hold has the power to transform your relationship with God. That's worth celebrating! So first I want to acknowledge you and the commitment you made to meet regularly with God.

In addition to my gratitude to God for every bit of grace and truth he has spoken into my life, I would like to thank the many others who took part in this work with me.

To the talented team who helped me with all the things that stressed me out: Jennie Scott, Katy Epling, and Sara Ward. Thank you for using your gifts for this project.

A special thank you to my writing mastermind: Cyndee Ownbey, Eva Kubasiak, Jazmin Frank, Katy Epling, Kristin Vanderlip, Sara Ward, and Thelma Nienhuis. Your presence makes this work less lonely and inspires me to keep going.

Thanks also to my extended writing community of hope*writers who supported me through endorsing and sharing this journal. And thank you to my early readers who provided such valuable feedback and helped shape these journals into what they are today.

My beautiful, kind, life-giving kids: Emery, Mia, Tessa, and Lincoln. You teach me every day what it means to love as Jesus does. These journals are for you. May they draw you closer to God and allow the Holy Spirit to comfort, guide, and encourage you no matter what you face in the years to come.

Finally, to my husband, Tynan. For a writer who can string sentences together for a living, words fail me in my deep love for you. I choose you every day.

About the Author

Taryn Nergaard is an author and life coach with a passion for helping people find freedom. She is the creator of the *Reflective Bible Journals*, which help kids, teens, and adults hear God's voice and follow his lead. In her years leading a healing-discipleship ministry, she discovered that very few people know what true freedom in Christ feels like. She wants to change that. Taryn believes that surrender is the pathway to freedom, and when we stop holding on to what's holding us back, we experience more hope, joy, peace, and purpose.

Taryn lives in British Columbia, Canada with her husband and four kids. When she's not busy homeschooling or working, you'll find her enjoying a cup of coffee and a good book, or curled up on the couch binge watching her current favorite show.

@tarynnergaard
www.tarynnergaard.com

Made in the USA
Columbia, SC
13 January 2021